Behavior Coaching

A Step-by-Step Guide To Helping Your Child Improve Behavior At Home and At School

Scott E. Hall, PhD
Matt Pasquinilli

Asian Arts Center Press
6077 Far Hills Ave. #212
Dayton, Ohio 45459

Copyright © 2005

No part of this book may be used or reproduced in any manner whatsoever without written permission of the authors. For further information please contact:

Asian Arts Center Press
6077 Far Hills Ave. #212
Dayton, Ohio 45459

ISBN 0-9712146-1-1

First printing January 2005

This book is dedicated to Teachers, Parents, and Students. Students are the future of America, teachers and parents are responsible for shaping that future. Be patient, be kind, and be honest.

Acknowledgements

Matt Pasquinilli

Thank you to my students, their parents, and teachers for allowing me to learn and grow. Thank you Kingsley and Thiele for your patience with me and for your friendship. Thank you Debbie Spiegel for your hard work, dedication to our cause, and for your great support.

Scott E. Hall, PhD

To my family, University of Dayton, and the Asian Arts Center for their support and teaching of character.

Table of Contents

Coach's Clipboard

Introduction

"Sow a thought, and you reap an Act; sow an Act and you reap a Habit; sow a Habit, and you reap a Character; sow a Character, and you reap a Destiny."

Anonymous

Building a Successful Character Identity

The idea of living with character goes back to the time of Plato and Aristotle. It was and is the practice of knowing the good, loving the good, and doing the good. What is "the good?" The "good" are virtues. Things like honesty, integrity, self-discipline, compassion, perseverance, love, courage, faith, flexibility, trustworthiness, forgiveness, and selflessness. Jesus taught virtues, the Knights practiced virtues with their code of chivalry, and people have embraced virtues in various ways throughout time. So why is it important to think about and practice the virtues? Simple. It leads to a better sense of self, others, and life. Building an identity based on good character, and then living by that code, helps define who we are, how we live, and what others know about us.

Character does not come easy. It takes effort. Developing good character is an ongoing process. Much of how we live has been modeled for us. Parents, teachers, friends, and other well-meaning folks catch our eyes and ears while growing up. We follow their lead in how decisions are made and how we relate to others. Sometimes we witness good examples, and sometimes we do not. However, we always have the choice to build good character.

Character should not be viewed as either you possess it or you don't, but on the belief that each virtue exists in varying degrees of development. Developed virtues such as love, honesty, etc. represent your strength of character and are pivotal in building a healthy lifestyle. We'll call these positive virtues. Each virtue that is underdeveloped (e.g. hate, dishonesty) can give you problems in life if they are frequently practiced. Underdeveloped virtues, we'll call negative virtues, represent the harmful aspects of who we are, yet are important for us to know. Why is it important? We all have the capacity to practice positive or negative virtues – good or bad thoughts or behavior. It takes a conscious effort to live a life of good character while being on guard to the unhelpful influences in our lives.

Scott E. Hall, PhD

Coach's Secret

The night before a big game, my basketball coach would gather the team together for some last minute coaching. "The team we play tomorrow has a strong offense. When they pass the ball to number 21, you have to stop him from getting to the basket." Our team was pretty good and spent many serious hours practicing all the basics of the game. We had become very skilled at passing, rebounding, and shooting. The coach had done a great job of teaching the skills and keeping us focused during practice. By the week of the game, there was not much left for the coach to do but give us the strategy to be successful. He would give us specific instructions on how to apply the skills we had developed in the weeks leading up to the game. We did not always win, but the "night before" coaching sessions gave us confidence and a sense of security.

I have never met a child who wakes up in the morning and says, "I think I'll go to school today and get into trouble." Or, "During quiet reading time, I am going to talk to another student and get yelled at by the teacher." I have known many children who get in trouble so often at school that it looks like it was planned, but it is not.

A distractible child tends to get in trouble at school for not paying attention. The child who worries about other children accepting him tends to get into trouble for talking to his classmates at the wrong time. If a child is hyperactive, she might get in trouble for not staying in her seat or "not keeping her hands to herself." Whatever the inappropriate behavior or action, the child will often know that it was wrong to do after he gets into trouble, but as we know, "hindsight is 20/20."

When I work with a child who has behavior issues at school, I ask the teacher or parent for a brief list of specific behaviors. For example, if I am initially told that a child "has a hard time staying on task," I ask for a specific example in the recent past. "During math Jack played with his pencil and scribbled on his work sheet." This specific example gives me some information about when Jack lost focus, and what behaviors he needs to avoid in the future. When I meet with Jack, I can coach him to success by saying "Jack, your teacher said that yesterday during math you played with your pencil and scribbled on your work sheet." Then I'll say, "Jack, you have math again today, and I want you to look at the teacher and leave your pencil on the desk unless you are writing with it. If you find yourself playing with the pencil or scribbling on your sheet, put the pencil down and start looking at the teacher again." In my experience, it will take Jack several coaching sessions before he remembers not to play with the pencil and to look at the teacher instead.

You must consistently reinforce the coaching by asking your child what happened at

13

school every night when they get home. (Remember to ask specific questions and not just "How was school today?") If your child forgot to apply what he learned in your coaching session, don't yell or get angry, simply give more coaching. Remember Bobby Knight, the college basketball coach who abused his students? He won a lot of games, but at what cost? Is there a better way? I know there is, and the best coaches teach, inspire, and encourage their players to victory. You can do the same; just remember to be specific and consistent.

Matt Pasquinilli

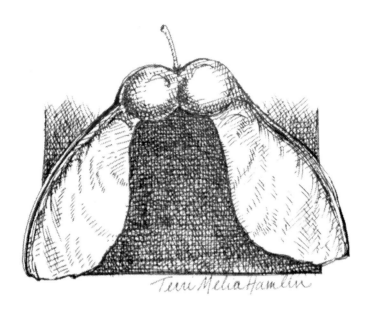

Terri Melia Hamlin

Behavior Coaching In 9 Steps

Through research and study, we have determined that all people desire to feel worthwhile, competent, and to be accepted into their peer groups. Our experience has shown that many of the negative behaviors that children exhibit at home and at school can be traced back to those three needs.

Believing that you don't matter or that you are not important can lead to feelings of depression and anger. Children who do not feel worthwhile often misbehave in order to get attention. Negative attention is better than no attention at all, and a child who causes a lot of disruption at school is getting tons of attention. After a while, the bad behavior becomes a habit that is hard to break; most importantly, if the behavior starts to improve, teachers and classmates have become so accustomed to the bad behavior that they miss the new behavior altogether.

When children become depressed because they don't feel worthwhile, they can become complacent and seem distracted. These children tend do the least amount of work possible and often slip through the cracks at a very young age. When they get older, their depression can cause them to hurt themselves or to lead a life of unfulfilled potential.

Competence is the quality of being able to do something well. When a child doesn't believe he is good at something, he experiences frustration and embarrassment. Misbehavior becomes a cover for thoughts of being dumb or weak. Some children misbehave more in math and not during reading. For other children it's reading and not math with which they struggle. This is not to say that all children who struggle will misbehave. If your child is misbehaving, then finding out when it happens during the day can be an essential factor in knowing how to address that behavior.

Belonging or "fitting in" gives comfort and security to children at every age. Not feeling acceptance will drive some children to constantly tattle on their classmates. While this seems counter intuitive (the classmates will reject his friendship even more than before), the motivation comes from seeking acceptance from the teacher. Other children might feel so insecure that they bully their classmates verbally and physically in an effort to create rejection on their own terms.

When we talk of "wellness" we refer to the way we think, feel, and behave. We all struggle in these areas from time to time and often need to change what we tell ourselves, how we feel, or what we do. Although we talk about thoughts, feelings, and behaviors separately, they are not mutually exclusive. In other words if a person changes their behavior they begin to think differently about themselves and thus feel differently. Likewise, if they change their attitude and thoughts about something then they will make different decisions about their behavior and feelings. Regardless of which part is the focus of change (thoughts, behavior, or feelings) any change will affect all three.

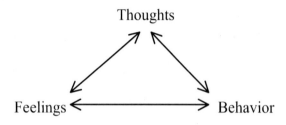

For example, suppose a child says after trying to throw a football, "I'm just a dummy, I can't throw a spiral." This is considered a negative self-statement (thought). However, it is the first part of the statement that is most damaging. The child has tied his worth as a person ("I'm just a dummy") to the failed attempt to throw a football. As a result, the child feels bad and will probably avoid throwing the football (behavior), especially around other people.

If the child says, "That wasn't a great throw, but I'll keep trying and will eventually throw it well," she begins to separate who she is from the kind of outcomes that will not always be in her control. She is a good person regardless of how she throws the football. She may not have liked how she threw the ball, but it did not make her a bad person. Sometimes children, and adults, need to reframe how they define success and failure, and begin to challenge their own negative self-talk. When they do so, they will feel less defeated and more willing to participate in challenging activities whether it is homework, sports, a job, or simple conversations.

Behavior Coaching utilizes many important attributes of positive parenting. Observation, discussion, and consistency are just three of the most crucial components of effective Behavior Coaching.

The following nine steps of Behavior Coaching will offer advice on how to better observe and discern the difference between actions and character, discuss with your child when and how to behave in a way that will keep her/him out of trouble, and follow up in a consistent manner. We have used these techniques and strategies with many children with great success, including many children with ADD/ADHD and Asperger's Syndrome.

This is a starting point for you, and as you begin this process and grow with your child, you will come up with what works best for both of you.

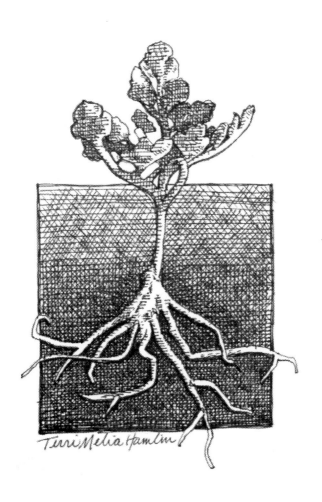

Terri Melia Hamlin

STEP 1 - Find A Good Time For Your Coaching Session

You need a time that works well for both of you. Having an important conversation when there are a lot of distractions will be stressful for you and your child. The likelihood for a successful outcome would be difficult. Try to find a time when you will not be interrupted by a ringing phone or a visitor at the door.

When scheduling your coaching session, consider your child's weekly or daily routine. If you schedule a time that interrupts a favorite television program or a time usually spent playing with a friend, you might spend the time fighting. A good time to talk might be half an hour before bed or just after dinner. About 30 minutes should be a sufficient amount of time. Much longer than 30 minutes might challenge your child's attention span and your patience. After a few coaching sessions, you will have a good idea of how much time is really required, and how often you should hold coaching sessions.

Step 1 Rules

- Time must be good for you
  and your child.

- Consider your child's daily
  and weekly routines

- 30 minutes is enough time

STEP 2 – Be Specific About What Behaviors Have To Be Changed

"Just the facts, Ma'am." That is one of my favorite lines from an old TV show, and it is highly applicable when discussing behavior with your child. You can only discuss what you see, not how you feel. I find it is very common for a parent to tell a child how a bad behavior makes the parent feel. Depending on the age of the child, this is ineffective at best, and at worst, it can have the effect of hardening a negative pattern of behavior. Sticking to the facts will allow you to have an unemotional interaction with your child and will increase the likelihood of you getting what you need.

Be specific. Start by writing out what the child is doing that needs to be modified before your coaching session. For example, you might write "throws a tantrum in the store when he doesn't get his way." This is a good start, but in order to change this behavior, you will need to be more exact. "When we were in the store yesterday, Andrew took a yellow ball from the shelf and stomped his feet and yelled 'you can't make me' when I told him to put it back." This is clear and precise, and Andrew will be able to recall the incident easier than if he is told, "You never listen to me," or "You don't do what you are told."

If you are coaching your child to behave better at school, you need to ask the teacher for specific behaviors and actions that your child is getting in trouble for. Teachers often avoid saying negative things about children and can use confusing terms to describe an inappropriate pattern of behavior. Recently, I heard a boy described by a teacher as being "spirited" and "highly social." What she really meant was that he got out of his seat a lot during class, and talked too much to other students. You need to pin down your child's teacher on exactly what actions or behaviors your child needs to change.

Once you have a list of behaviors you want to change, select one to start with. Tackle only one at a time. Trying to change too many behaviors at one time will be overwhelming and will cause frustration for you and for your child. Once your child changes one behavior, recognize him for it and move on to a new behavior. I like to start with the toughest behaviors first, and I have found that they are usually the easiest for a child to change.

Step 2 Rules

- Stick to what you see and not how you feel when discussing behavior

- Write down the specific behavior you want your child to change

- When school behavior is the issue, nail down the teacher on specifics

- Work on only one behavior at a time

STEP 3 – Physically and Mentally Prepare

"Take three deep breaths." Good advice, and perhaps the most common anger management tool used today. It doesn't work! Well, it does if you can remember to do it BEFORE you lose your temper. Breathing deeply has to be an automatic, conditioned response to stress in order for it to be helpful. As a parent, you need to be a master at breathing under stress if you want to remain calm and clearheaded when helping your child learn to change bad behavior.

You need to exercise. If not for yourself, then do it for your child. Exercise prepares the lungs for the deep breathing needed to reduce stress. In other words, once your heart races and your temperature rises, your body will naturally slow the heart and cool itself by breathing more fully and completely. You can walk, jog, do aerobics, go for a swim, whatever you can fit into your schedule. The rule is that it must be vigorous enough to raise the heart rate and increase the fullness of your breathing, and you must do it consistently for it to be helpful.

Once exercise becomes a part of your daily routine, you'll find yourself looking forward to this time set aside for yourself. Before long, you'll feel better, sleep better and find that you are more patient in dealing with your child's stressful behaviors on a day-to-day basis.

Meditation is also helpful. It can increase your peacefulness and train your body to take deep breaths. If you chose to meditate, you should look for a style of meditation that is simple and easy to practice. If you are successful in meditation, you should start to feel more calm and relaxed during the day. You can meditate shortly before your coaching session to help prepare you for the stress it might bring. If you don't want to read a lot of books about meditation or go to a meditation class, then try this: Sit comfortably with your eyes closed. Count to three slowly while inhaling, and then exhale to a slow count of three. Repeat until you feel more calm and relaxed.

Step 3 Rules

-You need to exercise on a regular basis

-You must be in good shape to breathe under stress

-Meditation can help relieve stress

STEP 4 – Suspend Judgment

Parents and teachers are often the "Judge, Jury, and Executioner" for misbehaving children. It is not all that obvious, but sometimes when a child has a pattern of negative behavior, a teacher or parent might think of that child as obnoxious, disrespectful, spoiled, or worse. It happens like this: The child says or does something that hurts or offends the adult. Somewhere in the back of that adult's mind, a judgment is made against the child's character and a subconscious decision is made to punish the child or to withhold trust from the child. Once judgment has been passed and a sentence handed down, it is very difficult for that child to make amends and to change the mind of the adult about his character. If you want to change a child's behavior, you must isolate the child's behavior and see it as a separate thing from the child's character.

You can change a behavior because it is based on actions. Character is more abstract, and it can be manipulated by changing behavior. Don't attack your child's value and self-worth by attacking their character. Recognize the behavior that needs to change and address only that behavior.

Step 4 Rules

-Separate your child's behavior from your emotions about that behavior

-Address behavior and not character

STEP 5 - Start Your Coaching Session With A Remark About Your Intentions And What You Hope To Get Out Of The Session

It is your job to raise a happy and healthy child. A parent that clearly defines boundaries and expectations will alleviate a lot of a child's stress. Happy children have less stress in their lives because they are not yelled at or punished as much. When you start your coaching session, let your child know that you are not mad and that you only want to help her become happier and healthier. This is a true statement, and it will help you establish and clearly define your role as the parent to your child and to yourself.

Help your child feel comfortable about the coaching session by smiling often and staying relaxed. If you start to feel frustrated or lose your place, take a quick break, get a drink of water, or take a short walk. Focus on your breathing to help you stay calm and in control. Once you are ready, you can call your child back and start again.

Step 5 Rules

-Tell your child that you are not angry

-Smile and stay relaxed

STEP 6 – Don't Do All Of The Talking

Be specific about what you want your child to do, and then ask them to repeat it. Ask a lot of questions, and listen to how your child answers. If you don't hear exactly what you are listening for, then try saying what you need to in a different way. It is easy to assume that you know what a child is thinking, but in reality, you only know what you hear them say.

Try to stay away from feelings and emotions. Avoid using shame to get them to do what they should be doing. Lay out what you want in a matter-of-fact way, and then stick to it. You don't always have to answer the question "why." Sometimes a child asks "why" in an attempt to "push your buttons." If the question is sincere and you think it is appropriate to answer, then explain why, but be concrete in your demand that your child follow the rule.

Ask your child how they see the situation that you are discussing. Listen closely to the answer, and don't correct what they are saying. Let them see you listening to their answer with the same attention that you want from them. When they say something you disagree with, say "I hear what you are saying," or "I understand your point." Avoid using the word but. When you say but, it

34

means that everything they said is wrong. Instead, use the word "**and**." "I hear what you are saying, **and** I know that your teacher would like you to raise your hand when you want to ask a question." "I understand your point, **and** I want you to understand that when we are in the store, you have to ask me before you take something from the shelf." In the end, you want to have a win/win solution, and it will come only when you listen to how your child sees and understands a situation.

Step 6 Rules

-Ask your child to repeat the main points that you are making

-Don't shame your child into agreeing with you

-Listen to your child with the same attentiveness you want from her

-Use "and" instead of "but"

STEP 7 – Give Good Alternatives to Negative Behaviors

Just telling your child not to act a certain way is not enough. It is always more helpful to tell someone how to act instead of how not to act. Using an example from earlier in this guide, you might tell Andrew, "Next time we are at the store and you really want something, I want you to point to it and say, 'Mom, I want that yellow ball.' If I say you can't have the ball, you might be disappointed, and I want you to take three deep breaths and say 'OK Mom.'" This may sound too simple, but it will give your child an alternative to grabbing the ball from the shelf and yelling when you tell him to put it back.

Ask them to come up with good alternatives to their bad habits. Listen to what they say, and don't dismiss their ideas if they are not appropriate or would not be practical. If their solution would not work in the situation, let them know, and then help them to better understand why. Try role-playing to help them understand what would happen with different alternatives. You might find that their alternatives are acceptable, and by letting them make suggestions, they will be more open to the change and will likely take greater ownership and responsibility for their behavior.

Write down all of the good alternatives that you and your child come up with. Writing them down makes them real for your child, and if your child is old enough, ask him to write them down. Once you have your list, you can refer to it every time you need to. You can even treat it like a legal document and refer to it to settle a dispute or argument. Challenge your child to think of more alternatives for the list later on. Put the list on the refrigerator or somewhere that your child will see it often. Give your child a copy of the list for his book bag or locker at school.

Step 7 Rules

-Tell your child "how to act" instead of "how not to act"

-Ask your child to suggest some good alternatives to negative behavior

-Write down all the alternatives and keep the list in a place it can be seen often

STEP 8 - Pre Game Pep Talk and Post Game Follow Up

Right before sending your child to the bus stop or dropping them off at school, have a brief "Pep Talk." This is just a reminder of what you talked about during the coaching session. Let your child know that they are about to face the situation that you talked about, and then remind them of how you want them to handle themselves. Tell them that after school is over, you will ask them for a full report. Let them know at this time that you will not be upset with them if they don't remember to use the strategies and alternate behaviors that you decided on during your coaching session. (It is important for you and for your child to know that habits are sometimes hard to break and that it might take time to make significant change occur. If you tell your child you won't get mad at him if this change has not taken place and then you lose your temper and show your frustration or anger, you will lose your credibility and your child's trust.)

When you pick them up or they come home from school, the first thing you should discuss is the specific behavior you talked about in the coaching session and that morning's pep talk. After greeting and welcoming your child, ask whether or not they faced the situation you have been working on. Be as specific as you were in the coaching session. Give them time to answer and sit silently while they think. Take deep and slow breaths to help control any emotional reaction you might have.

If your child reports that they did face the situation, but forgot to do what they should have done, then tell them that you will both keep working on it. If your child reports that they faced the situation, used the technique, but it did not help, then discuss the situation and try to determine where it might have gone wrong. Sometimes you will have to call the teacher and get the report from the teacher's perspective. Let the teacher know what you are doing at home and ask very specific questions about your child's behavior at school. It helps if you can let your child know what the teacher is observing and what the teacher needs to see in order to feel like your child is following the rules and demonstrating good and appropriate behavior.

Hopefully your child will start to report with real excitement that he had faced the situation and successfully applied the alternative behavior to it. Recognize this achievement, and ask a lot of questions about how easy or hard it was, how he felt when it happened, what the teacher may have said, etc. You want to help your child relive the experience so that you can deepen the significance of it. This builds your child's self-confidence and will let him see that he has control over his own behavior and thinking.

Step 8 Rules

-Give your child a brief "Pep Talk" right before she goes to school, the store, etc…

-Remind your child what she should do when facing the challenge you have been talking about

-Afterwards, ask your child what the outcome was from their changed behavior

STEP 9 – Celebrate!

I am a strong believer in applying praise and rewarding big accomplishments. Recognition of appropriate behavior can be more effective than praising for the sake of praising. Decide for yourself how significant a behavioral change is. If your child really fought hard to change a negative behavior, then celebrate big. If it is a small victory, then reward your child with something small and meaningful, but recognize him more with words than prizes.

A celebration is a big deal. Go out for ice cream, get your child the game he has been asking for, take a special trip to reward your child. Ask your child what they want as a reward for making a big change in her behavior. Recognition is simply saying that you saw progress or change. Simply say, "You are more focused at school." "Your teacher says that you are getting your class work done more quickly." "You look at me every time I talk to you." Add your "good job," or "keep up the good work" when it seems right.

You have to be careful not to make a big celebration for every little thing – it gets old and loses its effectiveness. Think of a song or a movie – if it were all one rhythm or speed, it would become monotonous and boring. If you constantly make a big deal of everything, there are no high or low points; all excitement and effect are lost. Most often, just knowing that you recognize the effort she is making, will be enough for your daughter to feel appreciated and valued. Save the big rewards for big accomplishments, and you will get more bang for your buck.

Step 9 Rules

-Celebrate big accomplishments

-Recognize small achievements

Behavior Coaching Summary

Preparing Your Coaching Environment

Choose a quiet, comfortable location
Work within a time frame that will be least
disruptive – keep your coaching session to within
30 minutes.

Preparing Yourself

Take deep breaths – in a comfortable position,
slowly breathe so that your belly rises and sinks as
you inhale and exhale.

Recognize that the action is a separate issue from
the child's character.

Addressing The Issue

Identify the actions and behaviors one behavior at
a time;   they should be based on the facts, and not
the emotions they create.

Beginning Your Coaching Session

Assure your child that you are not angry with him
or her.

Maintain a friendly, positive, and encouraging
coaching session.

Be specific when addressing productive solutions with your child.

Getting Feedback

Ask lots of questions.

Listen to your child's responses, being careful not to overcorrect what she/he has to say.

Repeat your child's responses.

Have your child repeat your intentions.

Use the word "and" instead of "but."

Creating Alternatives to Negative Behavior

Teach your child how TO act rather than how NOT to act.

Encourage your child to create his or her own alternative actions to negative behavior.

Write down these alternatives, or if your child is able, have him or her write these alternatives and *post them where they can be seen often.*

Testing the Method

When the moment arrives, discuss the list with your child.

Remind your child to do his or her best to adhere to the list as closely as possible when tempted to revert to the former inappropriate behavior.

Follow up with your child to assess the validity of the agreed-upon alternative methods.

Celebrating Your Child's Success

Praise the behavioral change no matter how big or small.

Tell your child what s/he did well by identifying the correct alternative method.

Causes of Negative Behavior

The following list shows some negative behaviors that might occur when your child is thinking and feeling less than worthwhile, competent, or accepted. Of course there may be many other reasons for negative behavior, such as boredom, a learning disability, emotional challenges, etc… This list is in no way complete, and is offered here as a starting point.

If your child feels less than **worthwhile**:

Attention seeking behavior

> Interrupting class with talking or noises
>
> Interrupting class by throwing something
>
> Interrupting class by hitting or inappropriately touching someone
>
> Interrupting class by "entertaining", or "clowning around"
>
> Falling out of seat
>
> Do the opposite of what the teachers says
>
> Acting sick or crying

Bad attitude and use of inappropriate language

Drug, alcohol and cigarette abuse

If your child feels less than **competent:**

Covering Up or Diverting Behavior

Daydreaming, sleeping

Disrupting class (see previous section)

Not "on task" during class work

Not turning in homework

Cheating

"Doodling" on paper instead of working

Fidgeting or playing with items on/in desk

Breaking the class rules

Breaking school rules

Cutting class

Vandalism

Theft

Passing notes.

If your child feels less than **accepted:**

Bullying

Pushing, hitting, kicking, pinching, and any other type of inappropriate physical touching

Calling classmates mean names

Making fun of others through imitation

Manipulating relationships (telling classmates not to play with other classmates)

Throwing things at classmates

Taking lunch money, toys, cupcakes, etc.

Behavior Coaching Checklist

❏ Find A Good Time For Your Coaching
     Session

❏ Be Specific About What Behaviors Have To
     Be Changed

❏ Physically and Mentally Prepare

❏ Suspend Judgment

❏ Start Your Coaching Session With A Remark
     About Your Intentions and What You Hope
     To Get Of The Session

❏ Don't Do All The Talking

❏ Give Good Alternatives to Negative
     Behaviors

❏ Pre Game Pep talk and Post Game Follow Up

❏ Celebrate

Coaching Character

Make a rule, and pray to God to help you to keep it, never, if possible, to lie down at night without being able to say: "I have made one human being at least a little wiser, or a little happier, or at least a little better this day."

Charles Kingsley

3 Steps to a Successful Character Identity
The steps are easy to list, but more challenging to do. To complete them requires positive virtue practice. You must be honest with yourself and persevere.

Step 1
Know the Good. *Gather information about yourself and the virtues you practice.* This includes positive and negative virtues. It is important to know which virtues help us (positive virtues), and which virtues hinder us (negative virtues). This knowledge shows our current character identity and provides a blueprint for necessary changes. For example, if your struggles in life are related to your practice of negative virtues, then you want to begin practicing the opposite positive virtues.

Step 2

Love the Good. *Value the information you gather and commit to positive virtues.* Use this knowledge to develop an attitude of acceptance toward positive virtues. Reflect on how the practice of positive virtues has helped you. Draw on your previous success with positive virtues and how your thoughts, feelings, and behavior are strengthened. Make a conscious decision to practice positive virtues at work, home, school, and community.

Step 3

Do the Good. *Practice positive virtues in your daily living.* Make a conscious decision to think and act in a positive way.

Actionable Definitions of Character For Children

Students who demonstrate good character are respected and admired by their parents, friends, peers, and teachers. Good character can be learned and practiced like most everything else your child does. Help your child build habits of good character by learning, practicing, and applying good character at home, at school, and with friends.

Actionable definitions of character are descriptions of behavior in terms of actions and words that can be easily understood and demonstrated by your child with consistency.

Use the following actionable definitions as a sort of script to discuss character with your child. Read the definitions word for word or rephrase them in the way that makes most sense to you.

Respect

To help your teacher and your parents feel respected, you have to pay attention, follow the rules, and do your own work. To help your friends feel like you respect them, be patient, be helpful and be kind.

SHOW RESPECT BY:

> Paying attention to your teacher or parents when they talk to you
>
> 1. Look in their eyes
> 2. Sit still
> 3. Think
>
> Follow the rules
> Do your own work
> Be patient with others

When you pay attention to your teacher and parents, do what your teacher and parents ask you to do, and follow the rules, your teacher and your parents will feel more respected. When you share and take turns, and when you are patient and courteous, your friends will feel respected.

Discipline/Self-discipline

Discipline is doing what you are told to do. Self-discipline is doing what you know you should be doing without being told to do it. You need both discipline and self-discipline to be successful at school and at home, or when playing sports or playing with friends.

Discipline: Do what you are told to do.

Self-Discipline: Do what you should be doing without being told.

Discipline:

> Do what you are told even when:
> > You don't want to
> > You are tired
> > You are grumpy

Self-Discipline:

> Do what you are supposed to do even when:
>
> > No one is watching
> > You can cheat
> > Your friends aren't

Focus

Look, be still, and think. You focus by looking at the person talking to you, standing or sitting still, and thinking about what they are saying. You can also focus on an activity using these same skills.

3 STEP FOCUS FORMULA

1. EYE CONTACT
2. BODY CONTROL
3. CONCENTRATION

FOCUS WHILE:

Your teacher is talking to you
Your parents are talking to you
Your grandparents are talking to you
Your friend is talking to you
You are doing your homework
You are working on a project
You are doing a chore
You are cleaning your room
You are brushing your teeth
You are practicing your sport
You are playing a game

Any time you are looking, controlling your body, and thinking about what you are doing, you are **focusing**.

Perseverance (Never Give Up)

When you face a challenge and you don't quit or give up, you are showing perseverance. Perseverance requires commitment, determination, courage, and persistence. Use the following formula to set and reach your goals with perseverance.

6 STEP PERSEVERANCE FORMULA

1. DECIDE WHAT YOU WANT
2. MAKE YOUR PLAN
3. TAKE ACTION
4. BE CONSISTENT
5. CHECK YOUR PROGRESS
6. REFUSE TO QUIT

REFUSE TO QUIT WHEN:

The task is difficult
You don't think you can win
Others tell you that you can't
You get bored or tired
You don't know how
The task seems long

Persevere in the face of a challenge by refusing to quit. When you face difficulty in completing a task or reaching your goals, take a deep breath, rethink your plan, and keep going.

Friendship

Some days it is easy to be friends with someone, and some days it isn't. Your friendships must be built on actions and on words. When you are having trouble with your friends, talk to them without showing anger and ask them questions. Listen to your friend's answers and find ways to meet your friend halfway when you disagree.

TALK TO YOUR FRIEND
LISTEN TO YOUR FRIEND
FIND COMMON GROUND
DO WHAT YOU SAY YOU WILL

SHOW FRIENDSHIP:

Share
Take Turns
Be patient
Be honest
Listen
Help
Be polite
Be caring

Share, take turns, and be patient with your classmates and you can become great friends. Friendship is more than feelings and emotions. Friends must be honest with each other and share what they are thinking and feeling.

Responsibility

All of our thoughts, words, and actions have consequences. Most of these consequences are positive and easy to accept. Sometimes we make mistakes and bad decisions, or are controlled by negative emotions and do the wrong thing. Sometimes we do the wrong thing and get in trouble without "meaning to." When you are aware of what is happening around you and know what you should be doing, you are better able to make the right decision and avoid getting in trouble.

Use the following formula to create awareness of your actions and accept their consequences whether they are good or bad.

ASK YOURSELF:

1. WHERE AM I?
2. WHAT AM I SUPPOSED TO BE DOING?
4. AM I DOING IT?

IF YOU ARE NOT DOING WHAT YOU SHOULD, THEN CHANGE RIGHT AWAY.

Honesty

Of all the character traits you need to possess to live your life with honor and self-discipline, honesty is the most important. For many people, honesty can be the hardest character trait because emotions get in the way of the truth. It is more important to be trusted and respected for being honest than to be liked for being dishonest.

BE HONEST:

> *With yourself*
> *With your friends*
> *With your family*

TELL THE TRUTH

> *When your teacher asks*
> *When your parents ask*

DO THE RIGHT THING

> *When your friends aren't*
> *When you can cheat*
> *When no one is watching*

Honesty with yourself and others can be hard when emotions get involved. You may be afraid of getting in trouble or losing a friend when you tell the truth. Being honest takes courage and strength.

Implementing actionable definitions in your child's daily life.

We have created small, easy to carry pocket journals that children use to log acts of character on a daily basis. These "Behavior Coaching Journals" serve to remind the child to work on a character trait every day and to record their progress. The act of recording good behavior shows the child that they are not always misbehaving, and so the log becomes an acknowledgment of their effort to change and improve.

We sometimes coach a parent or teacher to ask a child to "earn" a certain reward by filling in a journal over a brief period of time. The carrot and stick approach to changing behavior is flawed and outdated, but sometimes a privilege or reward can be a strong short-term motivator. You can make your own journal based on the actionable definitions we gave, or you can create your own definitions or examples to use.

Virtues of a Successful Character Identity: A Reflective Exercise

Define the following thirteen positive virtues of character for yourself. This exercise will help you to think in terms of concrete actions and words instead of thinking in hard-to-apply abstract terms. Also, to consider how you practice, value, encourage, model, and observe character. As you complete this task, seek out friends and family to discuss your answers, then seek to apply positive virtues in your daily living.

Respect
Love
Courage
Honesty
Faithful
Self-discipline
Perseverance
Flexibility
Responsibility
Compassion
Trustworthy
Selfless
Forgiving

Respect

"The best thing to give to your enemy is forgiveness; to an opponent, tolerance; to a friend, your heart; to your child, a good example; to a father, deference; to your mother, conduct that will make her proud of you; to yourself, respect; to all men, charity."

Francis Maitland Balfour

Answering the following questions will help you to better identify respect for yourself.

How do you show respect (to self and others)?

_____

When did showing respect help you?

_____

How do you handle disrespect (in self or from others)?

_____

How do you encourage others to be respectful?

_____

Love

"For one human being to love another; that is perhaps the most difficult of all our tasks, the ultimate, the last test and proof, the work for which all other work is but preparation."
- Rainer Maria Rilke

Answering the following questions will help you to better identify love for yourself.

How do you show love (to self and others)?

_____

When did showing love help you?

_____

How do you handle hate (in self or from others)?

_____

How do you encourage others to love?

_____

Courage

"Without courage there cannot be truth, and without truth there can be no other virtue."

- Scott E. Hall

Answering the following questions will help you to better identify courage for yourself.

How do you demonstrate courage?

_____

When did being courageous help you?

_____

When have you felt fear?

_____

How do you respond to cowardice (in self or others)?

_____

How do you encourage others to be courageous?

_____

Honesty

"Whatever games are played with us, we must play no games with ourselves, but deal in our privacy with the last honesty and truth."

Ralph Waldo Emerson

Answering the following questions will help you to better identify honesty for yourself.

How do you demonstrate honesty?

_____

When did being honest help you?

_____

How do you respond to dishonesty (in self or from others)?

_____

How do you encourage others to be honest?

_____

Faith

"This I do believe above all, especially in my times of greater discouragement, that I must believe – that I must believe in myself – that I must believe in my fellow men – and I must believe in God – if life is to have any meaning."

Margaret Chase Smith

Answering the following questions will help you to better identify faith for yourself.

How do you demonstrate faith?

_____

When did your faith help you?

_____

How do you respond to doubt (in self or from others)?

_____

How do you encourage faith in others?

_____

Self-Discipline

"What it lies in our power to do, it lies in our power not to do."

Aristotle

Answering the following questions will help you to better identify self-discipline for yourself.

How do you demonstrate self-discipline?

_____

When did being self-disciplined help you?

_____

How do you respond to undisciplined actions (in self or in others)?

_____

How do you encourage self-discipline in others?

_____

Perseverance

"Perseverance is more prevailing than violence; and many things which cannot be overcome when they are together, yield themselves up when taken little by little."

Plutarch

Answering the following questions will help you to better identify perseverance for yourself.

When have you persevered?

_____

When did persevering help you?

_____

How do you respond to idleness (in self or others)?

_____

How do you encourage others to persevere?

_____

Flexibility

"There is only one corner of the universe you can be certain of improving, and that is your own self."

Aldous Huxley

Answering the following questions will help you to better identify flexibility for yourself.

How do you demonstrate flexibility?

_____

When did being flexible help you?

_____

How do you respond to inflexibility (in self or from others)?

_____

How do you encourage others to be flexible?

_____

Responsibility

"Parents can only give good advice or put them on the right paths, but the final forming of a person's character lies in their own hands."

Ann Frank

Answering the following questions will help you to better identify responsibility for yourself.

How do you demonstrate responsibility?

_____

When did being responsible help you?

_____

How do you respond to irresponsibility (from self or others)?

_____

How do you encourage others to be responsible?

_____

Compassion

"Make a rule, and pray to God to help you to keep it, never, if possible, to lie down at night without being able to say: "I have made one human being at least a little wiser, or a little happier, or at least a little better this day."

Charles Kingsley

Answering the following questions will help you to better identify compassion for yourself.

How do you demonstrate compassion?

_____

When did showing compassion help you?

_____

How do you respond to cruelty (from self of by others)?

_____

How do you encourage others to be compassionate?

_____

Trustworthy

"Few things help an individual more than to place responsibility upon him, and to let him know that you trust him."

Booker T. Washington

Answering the following questions will help you to better identify trustworthiness for yourself.

How do you demonstrate being trustworthy?

_____

When did being trustworthy help you?

_____

How do you respond to being unreliable (from self or others)?

_____

How do you encourage others to be trustworthy?

_____

Selfless

"The way to get things done is not to mind who gets the credit of doing them"

Benjamin Jewett

Answering the following questions will help you to better identify selflessness for yourself.

How do you demonstrate selflessness?

_____

When did acting selfless help you?

_____

How do you respond to selfishness (in self and from others)?

_____

How do you encourage others to be selfless?

_____

Forgiving

"We must develop and maintain the capacity to forgive. He who is devoid of the power to forgive is devoid of the power of love. There is some good in the worst of us and some evil in the best of us. When we discover this, we are less prone to hate our enemies."

Dr. Martin Luther King, Jr.

Answering the following questions will help you to better identify forgiveness for yourself.

How do you demonstrate forgiveness?

_____

When did forgiving help you?

_____

How do you respond to resentment (from self or others)?

_____

How do you encourage others to forgive?

_____

Coach's Clipboard

This section contains actionable definitions of character traits and behavior, and checklists to use as tools in coaching your child for success.

Paying Attention or "Listen to Me"

Look at the person talking to you

Stand or sit still

Think about what the person talking to you is saying

Answering

Have your child respond to directions or comments you make by saying "yes Mom" or "yes Dad." This must become a habit for your child, and you must make sure you take the time to get a response when you talk. Ask questions to determine what your child does or does not understand from your discussion.

Discipline and Self-discipline

Doing what you are told to do without arguing and complaining is good discipline.

Doing what you know you should do without being told is good self-discipline.

Discipline sounds like this:

"Pay attention to me."

"Since you can't control yourself you have lost your recess."

"If I have to tell you one more time to stop talking, I am going to send you to the principal's office."

Self-Discipline sounds like this:

"Good eye contact."

"You are showing more control today than yesterday, you have really earned your recess."

"This is the second week in a row that you have been paying attention to me, and you have not interrupted me once when I was talking. Keep up the good work."

Self-Regulation Formula

Ask yourself the following three questions:

Where am I? (You need to know where you are in order to know what the rules are. In gym, the rules are different than in the classroom. At recess, the rules are different than in the music room.)

What should I be doing? (If you know what you should be doing, then you can check to see if you are doing it or not.)

Am I doing it? (If you are not doing what you know you should be doing, then quickly start doing it. This demonstrates self-control and puts you in charge of yourself.

Perseverance

Behavior change and growth takes a lot of work and can be very frustrating for you and your child. Remember these three keys to perseverance and teach them to your child when appropriate.

Don't ever quit (Always move toward what you want or need to do.)

Be patient (Big challenges and long journeys take time. Say, "I can't do it YET.")

Be nice (No one responds well to negative or mean comments. If you tell your child how awful they are or how dumb or stupid they are, your child will never get where they need to be. Most sane and loving parents would never do that to their child, but they often do it to themselves. If this sounds like you, tell yourself to stop the negative talk and only point out the positive things, or say nothing at all.)

Behavior Change

Handling stress in positive ways is the key to real behavior change. The body can be conditioned to handle the stress of exercise through breathing and controlled stretching. Once the body has been conditioned in this way, then the mind will tend to respond in the same way. For example, stopping in the middle of vigorous exercise and taking slow and full breaths while extending the arms and expanding the chest will condition the body to breathe when faced with physical or emotional stress.

Apply the Following Formula:

- Cleansing (clean out the body physically, through vigorous exercise and stretching)

- Learning (Learn better ways to handle stress and frustration)

- Training (Practice what you have learned so that it becomes a conditioned response)

- Application (Use your new techniques and strategies in response to stress and frustration)

Health and Diet Tips

From the US National Center for Chronic Disease Prevention and Health Promotion

Healthy Children, Healthy Choices

Parents are in charge!

As a parent, your responsibility is to buy healthy groceries and serve nutritious food to your growing children.

Start by establishing a routine, even if it is difficult at first. This means a set time for breakfast, lunch, dinner, and snacks. Once you have a routine for meals and snacks, meal times are more relaxed. Most children are happier on a schedule and become hungry at regular times. You'll feel happier about your parenting job when the family has a routine.

- So, be consistent! Children need a meal routine just like they need a bedtime routine. Plan for three meals and two snacks each day! Serve a vegetable or fruit at every meal. Fruits and vegetables are great for snacking too.

- Instead of rewarding your child with food, reward them with attention (hugs, kisses, and smiles) and playful activities.

Money-Saving Ideas For Better Health

- Avoid arguments about high-fat, high-sugar foods by not bringing them into the house. Leave the candy, soft drinks, chips, and cookies at the store.
- Serve water when your child is thirsty. Water is cheap and healthy.

Portion Size for Young Children 2–6 Years Old

Serve child-sized portions, and let your child ask for more. Here are some examples of child-sized portions:

- 1/3 to ½ cup of frozen veggies
- 1 or 2 little cooked broccoli spears
- ½ cup of tomato sauce
- 5 to 7 cooked baby carrots
- 1/3 to ½ cup of melon
- 5 to 7 strawberries
- ½ cup of apple sauce
- 1 small tangerine
- 1/3 to ½ cup of frozen or fresh berries
- 1 cup (8 fl. oz.) low-fat yogurt or nonfat milk

- 1/3 to ½ cup of macaroni-and-cheese, rice, pasta, or mashed potatoes
- 2oz. hamburger
- ¼ cup ground meat such as turkey or pork, browned and drained
- 1 or 2 drumsticks

TV Time

- Tired of hearing your children beg for sugary, high-fat foods? They may be influenced by too many commercials.
- Limit the amount of time your children watch TV to less than 2 hours a day. Remove the TV from your child's room.
- Find fun activities to do inside and outside your home: play hopscotch, jump rope, walk the dog, play hide-and-seek, or build an obstacle course in the hall.

Eat at Home

Part of having a healthy family includes spending time together. The family meal is a great way for everyone to get together, have a conversation, and eat together.

- Serving meals at home requires planning. Before you do your shopping, sit down and plan your meals for the week. Make a list of all the ingredients you'll need to prepare healthy, balanced meals. When fatigue kicks in and you want dinner on the table fast, your menu is already planned and the ingredients are right on hand.

- Make sure to always include low-fat or nonfat dairy products, fruit, and vegetables.
- Limit the amount of processed ready to-eat-snacks you buy (such as potato chips or cookies). Prepackaged and processed foods are usually higher in calories and fats and often more expensive. For the price of a large bag of chips and box of cookies you can buy the items below
    - 2 pounds of apples
    - 1 pound of bananas
    - 1 pound of carrots
    - 3 pounds of potatoes
    - 1 pound of peppers
- Simplify your schedule for better quality of life. Say no to lessons, teams, and commitments that don't interest you or your child. If you or your child are feeling overwhelmed, consider limiting the number of organized activities your child participates in to one per season.
- Children thrive on routine. Routine meals, naps, outdoor play, and bedtime can make for a happy child who comes to the table rested and hungry for the food you have prepared.

To serve a healthy and balanced meal at home, choose a variety of foods from several food groups. Children need to eat a variety of different foods every day. Use the USDA's Food Guide Pyramid for Young Children to help guide your food choices.

Getting Children Involved

An easy way to get children to try new foods is to get them involved in meals. Here are some age-appropriate suggestions.
3-year-olds can

- Wipe tabletops.
- Scrub and rinse fruit and vegetables.
- Wash and tear lettuce.
- Snap green beans.
- Bring ingredients from one place to another.
- Mix ingredients and pour liquids.
- Knead and shape yeast dough.
- Put things in the trash.
- Shake liquids in a covered container.

4-year-olds can also

- Peel oranges or hard cooked eggs.
- Mash bananas with a fork.
- Set a table.
- Cut parsley or green onions with kid-safe scissors.

5-year-olds can also

- Measure ingredients.
- Use an eggbeater or whisk.

Picky Eating Tips

- Parents are role models! Set a good example by eating healthy foods yourself! Buy and try new fruits and vegetables. Drink water between meals. Set an eating routine at home for your meals and snacks. Your children will learn by your good example.
- Don't expect your child to like something new the first time. Offer it again in a week. It usually takes several tries before children are willing to try new foods.
- Place a small amount of each food on your children's plates. Let them ask for more.
- It's normal for children to explore foods. Young children often touch or smell the food on their plate.
- Children thrive on routine. Just like you have a bedtime routine, stick to a feeding routine. Your child is less likely to be tired or fussy at mealtimes!
- Offer healthy foods. Your child soon learns these are the foods in your home and will eventually eat!

5 A Day Fruit and Vegetable Quick Tips

- Fruits and vegetables look good, taste great and contain vitamins and minerals.
- Eating 5 to 9 A Day is quick and easy. A serving is a medium-size piece of fruit; ¾ cup (6 fl. oz.) of 100 percent fruit or vegetable juice, ½ cup cooked or canned vegetables or fruit, 1 cup of raw leafy vegetables, ½ cup cooked dry peas or beans, or ¼ cup dried fruit.
- You can get your 5 to 9 A Day in many ways because fruits and vegetables come fresh, frozen, canned, dried, and as 100 percent fruit or vegetable juice.
- Wash fresh fruits and vegetables thoroughly in water.

How Many Servings Do You Need Each Day?

It depends on your age, gender, and activity level:

	Children ages 2–6 years old, women, some older adults	Older children, teen girls, active women, most men	Teen boys, active men
Calories	About 1,600	About 2,200	About 2,800
Vegetable Group	3 servings	4 servings	5 servings
Fruit Group	2 servings	3 servings	4 servings

*Adapted from the USDA Dietary Guidelines for Americans, 2000

Getting Started

- Not sure how to eat 5 to 9 A Day? Start the day with 100 percent fruit or vegetable juice. Slice bananas or strawberries on top of your cereal. Have a salad with lunch, and an apple for an afternoon snack. Include a vegetable with dinner and you already have 5 A Day. If you need more than 5 servings per day (see chart above), try adding a piece of fruit for a snack or an extra vegetable (like carrots or green beans) at dinner.

- There are so many choices when selecting fruits and vegetables. Have you ever tried kiwifruit? How about asparagus? Try something new that helps you reach your 5 to 9 A Day.
- Keep things fresh and interesting by combining fruits and vegetables of different flavors and colors, like red grapes with pineapple chunks, or cucumbers and red peppers.
- When you keep fruits and vegetables visible and easily accessible you tend to eat them more; for instance, store cut and cleaned produce at eye-level in the refrigerator, or keep a big bowl of fruit on the table.
- You can get some of your 5 to 9 A Day at restaurants too. Try some of these healthy choices.
  - Veggie pizza
  - Pasta with vegetables (but watch out for those high fat cream sauces)
  - Fresh vegetable "wrap"
  - Vegetable soup
  - Small salad (instead of fries)
  - Plenty of fresh vegetables from the salad bar.

In A Hurry During The 9 To 5? Pack And Go For 5 To 9 A Day!

- Buy ready-to-eat packaged fresh vegetables that are already cleaned. Pre-cut vegetables and salad mixes are a terrific 5 A Day time-saver. You'll find them at your local supermarket.
- A fast food alternative? Your local supermarket may offer prepared items, including sliced melons, fresh pineapple, salad mixes, and a salad bar to satisfy your hunger.
- Fruits and vegetables are nature's original fast food. When it's snack time, grab
  - Fruit— an apple or orange, or a zip lock bag and fill with sweet cherries, grapes, dried dates, figs, prunes, raisins, or apricots
  - Vegetables— carrot sticks, broccoli, or some red, yellow, and green pepper. Try dipping your vegetables in low-fat or non-fat salad dressing.
- In a hurry for a 5 A Day treat? Pick fruits and vegetables that require little peeling or chopping, like baby carrots, cherry tomatoes, cauliflower, grapes, apples, broccoli spears, an apple, a banana, or a box of 100 percent fruit or vegetable juice.
- Here's a great way to get some of your 5 to 9 A Day. Buy low-fat yogurt, fruit juice, and fresh, canned, or frozen fruit to blend a quick fruit smoothie. Get juicy! Buy 100

percent fruit or vegetable juice to quench your thirst and satisfy one serving of your 5 to 9 A Day.

Top Your Meals The 5 A Day Way

- Try these tasty additions to add flavor to your 5 A Day salad:
    - Green or red pepper strips, broccoli florets, carrot slices, or cucumber add crunch to your pasta or potato salad.
    - Baby carrots, shredded cabbage, or spinach leaves bring color to a green salad.
    - Apple chunks, pineapples, and raisins perk up coleslaw, chicken or tuna salads.
    - Oranges, grapefruit, or nectarine slices add extra flavor to any salad.
    - Fruit juice, flavored vinegars, or herbs make low-fat salad dressings flavorful without adding fat or salt.
    - Wake up with 5 A Day! Add sliced banana, blueberries, or raisins to cereal.
- Add fresh fruit and vegetables to foods you already eat — like berries and bananas to yogurt and cereal; vegetables to pasta and pizza; and lettuce, tomato and onion to sandwiches.
- Put some punch into your party by blending 100 percent fruit juices to create a

refreshing new juice. Try mixing pineapple, orange, grapefruit, or other fruit juices. Add a slice of lemon or lime as a garnish.

Cooking With 5 A Day

- Using a microwave is fast and fun. Use a microwave or pressure cooker to quickly "zap" vegetables or a potato and retain their nutrients.
- Grill fruits or vegetables. When grilling, wrap vegetables in aluminum foil, or use skewers of pineapple, yellow squash, eggplant, nectarines, zucchini, or cherry tomatoes, onions, and mushrooms. Place over medium-hot coals for a fun-to-eat and flavorful BBQ treat.
- Make a quick smoothie in the blender by puréeing peaches and/or nectarines, a touch of your favorite fruit juice, crushed ice, and a light sprinkling of nutmeg.
- Make homemade salsa with tomatoes, mangoes, avocados, red onions, cilantro, and limejuice.
- Looking for a fun appetizer when you entertain? Try making spears of fruit by attaching strawberries, grapes, melon slices, or pineapple chunks onto small skewers. Use low-fat or non-fat yogurt for a dip.
- Here's a quick fruit salad you can make in less than a minute. Open a can of juice-packed mandarin oranges and empty into a bowl. Add a sliced banana, a sliced apple,

and some blueberries or raisins. There you have it-a quick way to 5 A Day.

- Cool off with a great treat! Pour 100 percent fruit or vegetable juice into an ice cube tray or popsicle mold to make juice cubes or popsicles.
- Sometimes you can eat some of your 5 to 9 A Day in its' own container. Kiwifruit comes with its own serving cup and cantaloupe with its own serving bowl. Just cut them in half through the middle and scoop out each half with a spoon.

5 To 9 Fun For Kids

- Top off a bowl of cereal with a smiling face from sliced bananas for eyes, raisins for a nose, and an orange slice for a mouth.
- You can use broccoli florets for trees, carrots and celery for flowers, cauliflower for clouds, and a yellow squash for a sun. When you're all done, you can eat your masterpiece and get your recommended 5 A Day!
- Make frozen fruit kabobs for kids using pineapple chunks, bananas, grapes and berries.
- Go shopping with your children. Take them to the grocery store or farmers market to let them see all the different sizes and colors that fruit and vegetables offer. Let them pick out a new fruit and vegetable to try. By

making it fun and involving your kids, they'll be more likely to eat healthy foods.

Fitness Tips

From the US National Center for Chronic Disease Prevention and Health Promotion

Exercise (physical activity) helps build and maintain healthy bones, muscles, and joints; control weight; build lean muscle; reduce fat; prevent or delay the development of high blood pressure; and reduce blood pressure in some adolescents with hypertension.

Elementary school-aged children should accumulate at least 30 to 60 minutes of age-appropriate and developmentally appropriate physical activity from a variety of activities on all, or most, days of the week. An accumulation of more than 60 minutes, and up to several hours per day, of age-appropriate and developmentally appropriate activity is encouraged. Adolescents should engage in three or more sessions per week of activities that last 20 minutes or more at a time and that require moderate to vigorous levels of exertion.

Coach's Fitness Tips

Walking is great exercise and in addition, it gives you an opportunity to spend quality time with your child to talk. Try walking as a family.

Spend between twenty and forty minutes exercising at a moderate or brisk pace in order to elevate the heart rate and build cardiovascular power.

Stretching helps to alleviate stress and strengthen the muscles, tendons, and ligaments. Spend five to twenty minutes stretching the whole body. Yoga and Pilates style workouts are great for stretching the body.

Workout Videos and DVDs can be borrowed at your local library, or you can invest a small amount of money and purchase some to use at home. Your child might enjoy doing the workout with you, or you might prefer to exercise alone. Either way is fine, and the most important thing is that you are working out.

Joining a YMCA or YWCA or another local community fitness center is a great way to keep the whole family in shape. These family-focused facilities tend to offer many different types of physical programs for all ages and fitness levels. The key is to take some action and get started.

Be an underachiever. Instead of setting yourself up for failure with impossible goals, start as small as possible by committing to exercise for five or ten minutes a day. If you can exercise consistently for a brief period of time daily, then you will feel good about your accomplishment and will be more likely to add time later.

The Following is excerpted from the US government's Center for Disease Control and Prevention Website.

What is AD/HD?

According to the 2000 American Psychiatric Association's Diagnostic and Statistical Manual, Text Revision, of Mental Disorders-IV (DSM-IV-TR), ADHD is a Disruptive Behavior Disorder characterized by on-going inattention and/or hyperactivity-impulsivity occurring in several settings and more frequently and severely than is typical for individuals in the same stage of development. Symptoms begin before age 7 years and can cause serious difficulties in home, school or work life. ADHD can be managed through behavioral or medical interventions, or a combination of the two.

The year 2000 Diagnostic & Statistical Manual for Mental Disorders (DSM-IV-TR) provides criteria for diagnosing ADHD. The criteria are presented here in modified form in order to make them more accessible to the general public. They are listed here for information purposes and should be used only by trained health care providers to diagnose or treat ADHD.

DSM-IV Criteria for ADHD

Either A or B:

A. Six or more of the following symptoms of inattention have been present for at least 6 months to a point that is disruptive and inappropriate for developmental level:

Inattention

1. Often does not give close attention to details or makes careless mistakes in schoolwork, work, or other activities.
2. Often has trouble keeping attention on tasks or play activities.
3. Often does not seem to listen when spoken to directly.
4. Often does not follow instructions and fails to finish schoolwork, chores, or duties in the workplace (not due to oppositional behavior or failure to understand instructions).
5. Often has trouble organizing activities.
6. Often avoids, dislikes, or doesn't want to do things that take a lot of mental effort for a long period of time (such as schoolwork or homework).
7. Often loses things needed for tasks and activities (e.g. toys, school assignments, pencils, books, or tools).

8. Is often easily distracted.
9. Is often forgetful in daily activities.

B. Six or more of the following symptoms of hyperactivity-impulsivity have been present for at least 6 months to an extent that is disruptive and inappropriate for developmental level:

Hyperactivity

1. Often fidgets with hands or feet or squirms in seat.
2. Often gets up from seat when remaining in seat is expected.
3. Often runs about or climbs when and where it is not appropriate (adolescents or adults may feel very restless).
4. Often has trouble playing or enjoying leisure activities quietly.
5. Is often "on the go" or often acts as if "driven by a motor".
6. Often talks excessively.

Impulsivity

1. Often blurts out answers before questions have been finished.
2. Often has trouble waiting one's turn.
3. Often interrupts or intrudes on others (e.g., butts into conversations or games).

I.   Some symptoms that cause impairment were present before age 7 years.

II. Some impairment from the symptoms is present in two or more settings (e.g. at school/work and at home).

III. There must be clear evidence of significant impairment in social, school, or work functioning.

IV. The symptoms do not happen only during the course of a Pervasive Developmental Disorder, Schizophrenia, or other Psychotic Disorder. The symptoms are not better accounted for by another mental disorder (e.g. Mood Disorder, Anxiety Disorder, Dissociative Disorder, or a Personality Disorder).

Based on these criteria, three types of ADHD are identified:

1. ADHD, *Combined Type*: if both criteria 1A and 1B are met for the past 6 months

2. ADHD, *Predominantly Inattentive Type*: if criterion 1A is met but criterion 1B is not met for the past six months

3. ADHD, *Predominantly Hyperactive-Impulsive Type*: if Criterion 1B is met but Criterion 1A is not met for the past six months.

American Psychiatric Association: Diagnostic and Statistical Manual of Mental Disorders, Fourth Edition, Text Revision. Washington, DC, American Psychiatric Association, 2000.

Peer Relationships and ADHD

Attention-Deficit/Hyperactivity Disorder (ADHD) can have many effects on a child's development. It can make childhood friendships, or peer relationships, very difficult. These relationships contribute to children's immediate happiness and may be very important to their long-term development.

- Research suggests that children with difficulty in their peer relationships, for example, being rejected by peers or not having a close friends. In some cases, children with peer problems may also be at higher risk for anxiety, behavioral and mood disorders, substance abuse and delinquency as teenagers.
- Parents of children with ADHD may be less likely to report that their child plays with groups of friends or is involved in after-school activities, and half as likely to report that their child has many good friends. Parents of children with ADHD may be more than twice as likely than other parents to report that their child is picked on at school or has trouble getting along with other children.

How does ADHD interfere with peer relationships?

Exactly how ADHD contributes to social problems is not fully understood. Several studies have found that children with predominantly inattentive ADHD may be perceived as shy or withdrawn by their peers. Research strongly indicates that aggressive behavior in children with symptoms of impulsivity/hyperactivity may play a significant role in peer rejection. In addition, other behavioral disorders often occur along with ADHD. Children with ADHD and other disorders appear to face greater impairments in their relationships with peers.

Having ADHD does not mean a person has to have poor peer relationships.

Not everyone with ADHD has difficulty getting along with others. For those who do, many things can be done to improve the person's relationships. The earlier a child's difficulties with peers are noticed, the more successful intervention may be. Although researchers have not provided definitive answers, some things parents might consider as they help their child build and strengthen peer relationships are:

- Recognize the importance of healthy peer relationships for children. These relationships can be just as important as grades to school success.

- Maintain on-going communication with people who play important roles in your child's life (such as teachers, school counselors, after-school activity leaders, health care providers, etc.). Keep updated on your child's social development in community and school settings.

- Involve your child in activities with his or her peers. Communicate with other parents, sports coaches and other involved adults about any progress or problems that may develop with your child.

- Peer programs can be helpful, particularly for older children and teenagers. Schools and communities often have such programs available. You may want to discuss the possibility of your child's participation with program directors and your child's care providers.

The Following is excerpted from the US government's Center for Disease Control and Prevention Website.

About Autism

Autism spectrum disorders (ASDs) are a group of developmental disabilities that are caused by an abnormality in the brain. People with ASDs tend to have problems with social and communication skills. They also are likely to repeat certain behaviors and to not want change in their daily activities. Many people with ASDs also have unusual ways of learning, paying attention, or reacting to different sensations. ASDs begin during childhood and last throughout a person's life.

The following question and answer section will help you learn more about ASDs.

- What are some of the symptoms of ASDs?
- What conditions are included in ASDs?
- How common are ASDs?
- What causes ASDs? Can they be treated?
- Where can I go to learn more about ASDs?

What are some of the symptoms of ASDs?

As the name "autism spectrum disorder" says, ASDs cover a wide range of behaviors and abilities. People who have ASDs, like all people, differ greatly in the way they act and what they can do. No two people with ASDs will have the same symptoms. A symptom might be mild in one person and severe in another person. Some examples of the types of problems and behaviors a child or adult with an ASD might have follow.

- **Social skills:** People with ASDs might not interact with others the way most people do, or they might not be interested in other people at all. People with ASDs might not make eye contact and might just want to be alone. They might have trouble understanding other people's feelings or talking about their own feelings. Children with ASDs might not like to be held or cuddled, or might cuddle only when they want to. Some people with ASDs might not seem to notice when other people try to talk to them. Others might be very interested in people, but not know how to talk, play, or relate to them.

- **Speech, language, communication:** About 40% of children with ASDs do not talk at all. Others have echolalia, which is when they repeat back something that was said to them. The repeated words might be said right away or at a later time. For example, if you ask someone with an ASD,

"Do you want some juice?" he or she will repeat "Do you want some juice?" instead of answering your question. Or a person might repeat a television ad heard sometime in the past. People with ASDs might not understand gestures such as waving goodbye. They might say "I" when they mean "you", or vice versa. Their voices might sound flat and it might seem like they cannot control how loudly or softly they talk. People with ASDs might stand too close to the people they are talking to, or might stick with one topic of conversation for too long. Some people with ASDs can speak well and know a lot of words, but have a hard time listening to what other people say. They might talk a lot about something they really like, rather than have a back-and-forth conversation with someone.

- **Repeated behaviors and routines:** People with ASDs might repeat actions over and over again. They might want to have routines where things stay the same so they know what to expect. They might have trouble if family routines change. For example, if a child is used to washing his or her face before dressing for bed, he or she might become very upset if asked to change the order and dress first and then wash.

Children with ASDs develop differently from other children. Children without ASDs develop at about the same rate in areas of development such as motor, language, cognitive, and social skills. Children with ASDs develop at different rates in different areas of growth. They might have large delays in language, social, and cognitive skills, while their motor skills might be about the same as other children their age. They might be very good at things like putting puzzles together or solving computer problems, but not very good at some things most people think are easy, like talking or making friends. Children with ASDs might also learn a hard skill before they learn an easy one. For example, a child might be able to read long words, but not be able to tell you what sound a "b" makes. A child might also learn a skill and then lose it. For example, a child may be able to say many words, but later stop talking altogether.

Sources:
Mauk JE, Reber M, Batshaw ML. Autism and other pervasive developmental disorders (4th edition). In: ML Batshaw, editor. Children with disabilities. Baltimore: Paul H. Brookes; 1997.
Powers MD. What is autism? In: MD Powers, editor. Children with autism: a parents' guide, 2nd edition. Bethesda, MD: Woodbine House; 2000. pp. 1-44.

What conditions are included in ASDs?

ASDs include autistic disorder, pervasive developmental disorder - not otherwise specified (PDD-NOS, including atypical autism), and Asperger disorder. These three conditions all have some of the same symptoms, but they differ in terms of when the symptoms start, how fast they appear, how severe they are, and their exact nature. These three conditions, along with Rett syndrome and childhood disintegrative disorder, make up the broad diagnosis category of pervasive developmental disorders.

How common are ASDs?

We at CDC do not know how many people in the United States have ASDs. We do know more about children with ASDs than about adults with ASDs. Studies done in Europe and Asia since 1985 have found that as many as 6 of every 1,000 children have at least one ASD. We do have information about how common ASDs are in children in some parts of the United States.

We track the number of children with ASDs and four other disabilities in a five-county area in metropolitan Atlanta (Georgia) through the Metropolitan Atlanta Developmental Disabilities Surveillance Program (MADDSP). In 1996, 3.4 of every 1,000 children 3 through 10 years of age in metropolitan Atlanta had at least one ASD.

We have also studied how common ASDs were in Brick Township, New Jersey, in 1998. We found that 6.7 of every 1,000 children 3 through 10 years of age had at least one ASD.

We are now working with several states to learn how many children in other parts of the country have ASDs. These states are developing or improving programs that track the number of children in their areas with ASDs. The program,s began gathering information in 2002, and we expect that they will start reporting findings in late 2003.

We also know that in the United States during the 2000-2001 school year, more than 15,000 children 3 through 5 years of age and more than 78,000 children and adults 6 through 21 years of age were classified as having autism under the Individuals with Disabilities Education Act (IDEA). IDEA is the federal law that supports special education and related services for children and youth with disabilities. However, there are more children with ASDs who are classified under IDEA in a disability category other than autism. There are, however, some children with ASDs who are not included in these counts, such as children who are in regular education classes, who attend private school, or who are home schooled.

We do not know if ASDs are becoming more common in the United States. We do know that today more children are being identified as having an ASD than in the past. The studies that have looked at how common ASDs are often used different ways to identify children with ASDs, and it is possible that researchers have just gotten better at identifying these children. It is also possible that professionals know more about ASDs now and are therefore more likely to diagnose them correctly. Also, a wider range of people are now being classified as having ASDs, including people with very good language and thinking skills in some areas who have unusual ways of interacting or behaving. Clearly, we have much more to learn.

CDC studies in Atlanta and CDC-funded studies in the states will continue over time and will help answer this important question of whether ASDs are truly becoming more common in the United States.

What causes ASDs? Can they be treated?

No one knows exactly what causes ASDs, but scientists think that both genetic and environmental factors might play a role. We do know that parental actions do not cause children to have ASDs. We are now planning the Children's Longitudinal Development Study (CHILD Study), which will look at what factors make it more likely that a child will have an ASD. We are also funding several state projects that will study such factors.

If you would like to learn more about a specific genetic condition that you think could cause an ASD, you can go to the National Library of Medicine's Genetics Home Reference Web site. Information on each genetic condition includes symptoms, how common it is, related genes, treatments, and links to resources where you can learn more about the condition. The Genetics Home Reference also can help you learn more about genetics, including genetic testing, genetic counseling, and gene therapy.

There is no known cure for ASDs. However, early and intensive education can help children grow and learn new skills. The goal of these efforts is to help with the difficult symptoms of an ASD in a child and to improve the child's skills that help him or her talk, interact, play, learn, and care for his or her needs. Medicines can relieve symptoms and be helpful for some people, but structured teaching of skills (often called behavioral intervention) is currently the most effective treatment.

Sources:

Mauk JE, Reber M, Batshaw ML. Autism and other pervasive developmental disorders, 4th edition. In: ML Batshaw, editor. Children with disabilities. Baltimore: Paul H. Brookes; 1997.

Powers MD. What is autism? In: MD Powers, editor. Children with autism: a parents' guide, 2nd edition. Bethesda, MD: Woodbine House; 2000. pp. 1-44.

Journal

Journaling is not only a way to keep track of your progress, it also serves as a record of what was said and when it was said. This information is essential in trying to figure out what you are doing well and what you might need to change or get help with.

Tracking your conversations on the following pages will help you better understand your role in the coaching process. Be specific about what you are thinking and what you want to say to your child. Writing this out will help you organize your thoughts and help you return to the main points you want to cover if you find yourself lost in a tangent or argument.

Journal Page   Date

Write down what you need to discuss. Take notes
regarding your conversation. Remember to discuss
behaviors and not emotions or character.

Behavior you need to discuss:

_____

What does it look like (what actions is your
son/daughter taking that are inappropriate?)

_____

When do these actions happen (what time/place?)

_____

What alternative actions are more appropriate (what
should your son/daughter be saying or doing
instead?)

_____

_____

Follow up notes:

_____

_____

_____

Journal Page   Date

Write down what you need to discuss. Take notes
regarding your conversation. Remember to discuss
behaviors and not emotions or character.

Behavior you need to discuss:

_____

What does it look like (what actions is your
son/daughter taking that are inappropriate?)

_____

When do these actions happen (what time/place?)

_____

What alternative actions are more appropriate (what
should your son/daughter be saying or doing
instead?)

_____

_____

Follow up notes:

_____

_____

_____

Journal Page   **Date**

Write down what you need to discuss. Take notes
regarding your conversation. Remember to discuss
behaviors and not emotions or character.

Behavior you need to discuss:

_____

What does it look like (what actions is your
son/daughter taking that are inappropriate?)

_____

When do these actions happen (what time/place?)

_____

What alternative actions are more appropriate (what
should your son/daughter be saying or doing
instead?)

_____

_____

Follow up notes:

_____

_____

_____

Journal Page   Date

Write down what you need to discuss. Take notes
regarding your conversation. Remember to discuss
behaviors and not emotions or character.

Behavior you need to discuss:

_____

What does it look like (what actions is your
son/daughter taking that are inappropriate?)

_____

When do these actions happen (what time/place?)

_____

What alternative actions are more appropriate (what
should your son/daughter be saying or doing
instead?)

_____

_____

Follow up notes:

_____

_____

_____

Journal Page   Date

Write down what you need to discuss. Take notes
regarding your conversation. Remember to discuss
behaviors and not emotions or character.

Behavior you need to discuss:

_____

What does it look like (what actions is your
son/daughter taking that are inappropriate?)

_____

When do these actions happen (what time/place?)

_____

What alternative actions are more appropriate (what
should your son/daughter be saying or doing
instead?)

_____

_____

Follow up notes:

_____

_____

_____

Journal Page   Date

Write down what you need to discuss. Take notes regarding your conversation. Remember to discuss behaviors and not emotions or character.

Behavior you need to discuss:

_____

What does it look like (what actions is your son/daughter taking that are inappropriate?)

_____

When do these actions happen (what time/place?)

_____

What alternative actions are more appropriate (what should your son/daughter be saying or doing instead?)

_____

_____

Follow up notes:

_____

_____

_____

Journal Page   **Date**

Write down what you need to discuss. Take notes regarding your conversation. Remember to discuss behaviors and not emotions or character.

Behavior you need to discuss:

_____

What does it look like (what actions is your son/daughter taking that are inappropriate?)

_____

When do these actions happen (what time/place?)

_____

What alternative actions are more appropriate (what should your son/daughter be saying or doing instead?)

_____

_____

Follow up notes:

_____

_____

_____

Journal Page   Date

Write down what you need to discuss. Take notes
regarding your conversation. Remember to discuss
behaviors and not emotions or character.

Behavior you need to discuss:

_____

What does it look like (what actions is your
son/daughter taking that are inappropriate?)

_____

When do these actions happen (what time/place?)

_____

What alternative actions are more appropriate (what
should your son/daughter be saying or doing
instead?)

_____

_____

Follow up notes:

_____

_____

_____

Journal Page   **Date**

Write down what you need to discuss. Take notes
regarding your conversation. Remember to discuss
behaviors and not emotions or character.

Behavior you need to discuss:

_____

What does it look like (what actions is your
son/daughter taking that are inappropriate?)

_____

When do these actions happen (what time/place?)

_____

What alternative actions are more appropriate (what
should your son/daughter be saying or doing
instead?)

_____

_____

Follow up notes:

_____

_____

_____

Journal Page   **Date**

Write down what you need to discuss. Take notes regarding your conversation. Remember to discuss behaviors and not emotions or character.

Behavior you need to discuss:

_____

What does it look like (what actions is your son/daughter taking that are inappropriate?)

_____

When do these actions happen (what time/place?)

_____

What alternative actions are more appropriate (what should your son/daughter be saying or doing instead?)

_____

_____

Follow up notes:

_____

_____

_____

Journal Page   **Date**

Write down what you need to discuss. Take notes
regarding your conversation. Remember to discuss
behaviors and not emotions or character.

Behavior you need to discuss:

_____

What does it look like (what actions is your
son/daughter taking that are inappropriate?)

_____

When do these actions happen (what time/place?)

_____

What alternative actions are more appropriate (what
should your son/daughter be saying or doing
instead?)

_____

_____

Follow up notes:

_____

_____

_____

Notes

_____

_____

_____

_____

_____

_____

_____

_____

_____

_____

_____

_____

_____

_____

_____

_____

_____

Notes

Notes

_____

_____

_____

_____

_____

_____

_____

_____

_____

_____

_____

_____

_____

_____

_____

Notes

Notes

Notes

Notes

Check out other publications by Matt Pasquinilli and Scott E. Hall at www.theteachingreport.com and www.theparentingreport.com. Purchase "The Child Whisperer" at www.pasquinilli.com or buy it on Amazon.com.

or send check to
Asian Arts Center Press
6077 Far Hills Ave #212
Dayton, Ohio 45459

Quantity		Amount
_____	$9.95	$_____
Ohio residents please add 7.5% sales tax		$_____
Shipping	$3.00	$_____
Additional copies	$1.00	$_____
Total amount enclosed		$_____

BEHAVIOR COACHING

A STEP-BY-STEP GUIDE TO HELPING YOUR CHILD IMPROVE BEHAVIOR AT HOME AND SCHOOL

Tools for parents and school teachers

Works well for ADD/ADHD behavior

Highly useful for children with Asperger's Syndrome

Simple to use techniques and strategies

The best gentle behavior modification from experts who use it everyday

Scott E. Hall, PhD
Matt Pasquinilli

For more copies of "Behavior Coaching", send check to:

Asian Arts Center Press
6077 Far Hills Ave #212
Dayton, Ohio 45459

Quantity		Amount
_____	$14.95	$_____
Ohio residents please add 7.5% sales tax		$_____
Shipping	$3.00	$_____
Additional copies	$1.00	$_____
Total amount enclosed		$_____

Scott E. Hall, PhD

Scott Hall is an Associate Professor in Counselor Education at the University of Dayton, a past president of the Ohio Counseling Association, and a Clinical Counselor in private practice. Dr. Hall's teaching and research interests focus on identity and character development and midlife transitions.

Dr. Hall can be reached at halls@udayton.edu

Matt Pasquinilli

Matt Pasquinilli is a Professional Educator and writer living in Dayton, Ohio. He teaches and advocates for children, and specializes in helping children with ADD/ADHD learn how to control themselves effectively and naturally. Matt's writing is for parents and educators of all children with or without special needs.

Matt Pasquinilli can be reached at pasquinilli@hotmail.com